Arthur Dies

First Chronicle: Heirs of Constantine
Vol. I

OLCHAR E. LINDSANN

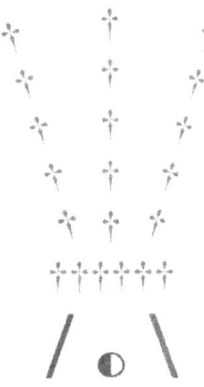

2015
LUNA BISONTE PRODS

Arthur Dies
First Chronicle: Heirs Of Constantine

VOL. I

© Olchar E. Lindsann 2015

~~~~~~~~~~~~~~~~~~~~~~~~~~~~~~

"rlin:
'Flee thou from the fire of the sons of Constantine, if flee thou mayst!
Even now they are fi "

-Geoffrey of Monmouth, *Historia Regum Britanniae*, Book VIII.

~~~~~~~~~~~~~~~~~~~~~~~~~~~~~~

Book design and cover collage by C. Mehrl Bennett

ISBN 978-1-938521-21-8

LUNA BISONTE PRODS
137 Leland Ave.
Columbus, OH 43214 USA

http://www.lulu.com/spotlight/lunabisonteprods

Exordium

~~~~~~
" nd wisse me to warp out   some word at this time
That nother void be ne vain   b
                [. . .]
                                   ghty
Herkenes me hendely   and holdes you stille,
And I shall t "
                     -*Alliterative Death of Arthur*
~~~~~~

Hwaet ,friends :hearken with your eye and earen both
            and i shall shadow forth the thane
who Was not once and shall not Be again in future time.
read, friends :letters hackstrew n o,n the bleache d fields
            si,lent to the scatt ered seeds, all dead.
hear ,friends :voice what was not once ,rhythmic ,sung
            lost battles caought within your throaten lungs.
Weep ,friends :for the dead you are to weep for
        Arthur ,dead as
            you shall die.

come to my **A**id o,tongue, or else the tongue of some
one other :sculpt the fântome from my ghosts of words
,let it be armoured by the teeth in bladesharp consonants
,bloodsinew animate with voweling trem,bled breath
:come to my aid give voice to what cannot be voi c,ed
,in music modulate send forth the shade
                    of Arthur
,of his sires ,thanes ,loves ,pains ,of pyres, births of deaths
let what refused to Be borne on your breath that dies,
        as you shall die
    ,as Arthur who
refused to live in death

v

Hwaet, **F**riends,

    so with my words i trace the crigat fate
of Albion ,that sleeps within all speech: nor that
c*truel* king dom prowling on the waves for blood and gold
and down whose walls the blood of warriors pants, in stead
i sing to you:
  some *other* Albion refused ,unborn to life
  some *other* Albion ,and dedicant to different strife
of which the Albion that is and that has been
is but a borted failure of, is but the rot. hwaet :*no*:
to los and enitharmon bound this *other* Albion:
that infrathin community that spans the brea*d*th
between eht Void of writing et the trawlats br*d*eath
of speech, from Thought to carnal pulse of nerve et blood
the realm that cannot be nor c,ease to be nor yet
refuse to be: lost Albion the ,always already dead
:the l,and of Arthur ,doomed between the wold of rot
and that of loss and dream ,dissemi nation
   :of those who think and yet Are not
  this Arthur was the -king ,o not a King
of rule but -king ,the ema nation manifest
of all the brythons unborn ,people of the gap.
    i write i sing of Arthur
   born for death and never dead
    i write i sing of Arthur
   guardian of keen impossibilities
    i write i sing of Arthur
   for his dream is dead, as he is
    i write i sing of Arthur
   hatching from the husk of tyrants
    i write i sing of Arthur
   against all states against
   his origins against all rule
   against the World against
   all history against the gods

         i write i sing of Albion
                in defi*n*ance in
                despair in rage
                in laughter in
                tears in mourning
           i write i sing of Albion
      of what is always lost of what
              was always lost of what
              we shall forever have
        already lost: i write i sing
    of who we were not, are, and shall not be
       :Hwaet: i sing out promise and o shame
in Albion in Arthur ,relict of the doom of thought.

Preface

~~~~~~~~~~~~~~~~~

" icies, when I cannot be sure of the interpretation thereof. It is good to keep my lips from speech, since the issue of events may make my gloss a lie.

                                                                The kin "

                -Wace, *Roman de Brut*.

~~~~~~~~~~~~

" itons loved him greatly,   and oft tell lies of him,
And say many things   about Arthur the king,
That took place never   in this earthly kingdom.
En

                      [. . .]
                    iant in everything,
For the truth stands in writing "

                         -Layamon, *Brut*.

~~~~~~~~~~~~~~~~~

Of failure, loss, and love i feign would speak,

and Arthur, that so distant lord of war-
ning and of lamentations:

                 How he sleeps

in silent cryptic avalon, the land
of death, undying, secreted in death's core
                                ,and hauntes
the borderlands thought tameless shadow, now
once passed, again, and imminent,
once always already, and always
        dying, waits,
                and never dies.

Of Arthur i would speak, who spurned his fate
and loved what could not be; and how he reaps
his future state in churning what has hapwise passed before,
suspend for what is *not* does not feed death
and so he waits, beloved as he is
of avalon which shimmers, voiding past
and wraps him all away from all that Is, and can be lost.

too Would i speak of diverse births
                           and let caress
with tongue of ink the diverse little deaths
and fleshless loves that ceaseless vaunt
has rendered ehtooms
                as *hierro*
to you that lust has to lithe,
                or loves that for to *ici*
and render many names to honours of much lesser fame
                of awke deedes,
,who struck
        with s'words of ancient lineage
,who spoke
        with cunning, weaved their tales cross
the wheel
        round which gathered
                in feasting song and contest all
                      who struggled gainst the World of death.

Of Arthur, adredde ay shame,
who strode doubly through the world, i wish to speak
and tell
        of he who from ashed ruins
                crafted well
        a realm of love; and so i seek

to say what was that city caerleon,
impossible, the city of the clinamen,
    wherein there lived what cannot live;

              And of

his willful s'word that gave
              to thought the force to form the
world against its morbid weft, and weave a nobler doom.

    and **L**ikewise would i speak of hapless wilds

    where dwell the tsaeb gnitseuq, where roams
    that bright kaleidoscopic clutch of steel,
    grim knights in gauded colours, shattered fields
where futures bleed into the thirsty loam,
              gutted like steel fish.

i would speak of Arthur,

          Child of treachery,

    who wrested sunshine from the *sodden* air
    who *nerved* the muscle to the dance of thought
    who carved away a narrow slice *from* time
        and planted there an intricate garden
    who tended for *a* season *a* wondrous thing
    who died.

        of Arthur i would speak,

but **T**rue it is the lies the people's bards

will sing will ever e at
              at board. The man is loa the,
and many breeds of lie abound, and some
will stin g
        and others, yalrap-messengers
,drag words of severed

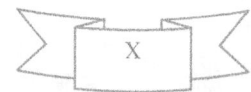

o,r magic heads.

to **A**rthur i would speak ,that distant -king
who lies beneath
                the waters
                       many lies
in avalon, where *speech*
                       shall never reach:
the rarified country,   fortunate isle,
        where *speech* is the dust of barrows.

and so of Arthur xud murolleb i
shall **W**rite:
      of Arthur,
          he who
                should ered   hope.

1: The Funeral of Constantine,

Father of Uther, father of Arthur.

I

~~~~~~~~~~~~~~~~~~~~~~~~~~~~~~~~~~

"ire to hold secret converse with him, when all had gone apart, slew him wi
[...]
s himself panting to snatch the crown at all haza"
-Geoffrey of Monmouth, *Historia.Regum Britanniae*, Book VI.

~~~~~~~~~~~~~~~~~~~~~~~~~~~~~~~~~~

two decades before arthur shall be born, the assembled hosts of the brythons assemble for the great funeral of constantine, pen-dragon of Albion, who has been slain by poison from an unknown hand. assailed by enemies on all sides and torn from within by suspicion and greed, Albion has stood against the World of death since constantine and vivienne, grasping the sword and the laurel of dying rome, united the tribes in common defense. now, with constantine murdered by a treacherous unknown hand, his widow vivienne guards with drawn knife her three young children: the youngest, uther, passionate and impulsive; ambrosius-merlinus, of enigmatic mien; and cautious vortigern, constantine's chosen heir. meanwhile, constantine has been interred and surrounded by the sacred talismans of Albion, in the great barrow of his ancestors at amesbury, where his body awaits the final words of his family before his tomb is sealed and his people perform the great dance around his balefire to usher him toward the Void.

        Convulsive in the bowels of rotting rome
it writhed: doomed albion, lamentable wretch
                ed like a nest of maggots
          frantic for the noisome flesh.

      on the wind the moarns of Urizon
           cut like squirm ed howls:

    for Constantine,
           the pen-dragon
was dead, the ghost of rome,
        which he had killed himself
        and rome was dead in him, and all about
the World pressed in against them, and a bounding fear
          conceived by plunging spears,

                    enwombed and birthed
            by human tongues:
                        for from the north
            poured down the *picts*, their skin abloom
    with florid curls of ink blue cigam rune
        ,their speartips hsrah their warcries keened awag
                whilst from the west
in ships like shadows gliding oer the flametipped waves
        of sun-drowned seas came crashing on the crests
        the *gaels*—racketing, in rush; in rout
        the *brythons* wasted, withering:
                            in doubt

for **S**truck by subtle *shamesdeede* choking *poison* wraglat phgm
the -king had gag;ged sa slaking agony his
                            spittle was,ting
            noi sesome wratch
                    {the silent
                        who?
    }in the midst of lamentable troubles
    vomited his life upon the stones
                    who
        had thus decanted from a vile *philtre*
        catastrophe to Albion?
                        no thane
        nor pict nor gael nor granulous pretender
        proclaimed the deed, nor deemed to profit thus,
nor claimed the throne, but all were crouched and glared askance
                evaid by sourceless death
    whilst murder sealed its sseldulb lips
                            and whispers vouched
    that sklein immortal Molech, named as Gwyn-ap-Nudd
        enmasked and clothed by lovely Ashtoroth,
            deitic child of violence
        himself had hunted Constantine
        for pure delight in dealing cards of death;
        and all the thanes, both men and women, wept

with eyes as dry as dnas
for fear of silent daggers in the dusk
more shoun for the swap of grisped s'words
than for the cerihabities of mourning
and all awatch with gleaming dread and searing jealous agita
        tion   *each on each*
the air aswim with pregnant
threat, as if the breeze were bristling blades
    and all the dew astrewn with blood.

and so the brythons **R**aised a bulging barrow ,hunched

    against the seeping sky, as armies l urched
    and drifted crost the skin of Albion
    with shallow breaths.
        like moths the thanes
wound nigh the place where gaping, yawned the mound
    of Constantine, dead -king, and treachery
    surrounding, roundabout a ring of kin
    -dling, beacons to the Zoa,
        waiting, bound
    in fronds of cyprus.
        weeping, **V**ivienne
the queen watched wary whilst the wall of loam
grew bulking,
        royal feast-hall for the worms,
and waited for the day of funeral,
her knife
    aglint
        in sleep and waking, lit
with embers glimmering, and all athirst
    for traitors blood. and clutched to her
in raesf curl sorrow burning lashyard agony
    three children: Uther, Vortigern, and dark
    Ambrosius-ap-merlin:
        huddled close

and all too young to bear the weight
				of doom.

	so midst the Twilight of his final dance
	,deep in his barrow Constantine declined
	in gray and sunken death, his earth-choaked womb
			enclosed in silence slight;
	his face half-shadowed
			by *Wyrmwhit,* Helm of Albion
				,its pallid mask of wan-gold;
	his fists enlaced apommel
			of *Caliburn,* S'word of Albion
				,its blade swift coursing steel;
	his shoulder stoutstraped
			to *Dargwythievoder,* sheltring shield of Albion
				,its battered skin a maze of scars;
	his armgrip crooked the shaft
			of *Rhongomyniad,* grim Spear of Albion
				,its pinion keen to pierce
	the darkness, all coagulate—
				and yet
		above the unseen skies were laced
	with blazing fires with drumbeats bashed, the hide
	of cattle, meat of cattle spiced the sky
across, the pounding of the dauncers feet on dirt
and darts of grim mis*t*rust that tweaked the smoke the
			prayers et pyres
		,*fumé* snakes flinching in the winds,
					the stars
	aglint .atop
			the deathmound-crest there raged
	the fierous flame addressed to claeven Los,
	its heart aboil with a lethal light
			whose flickered arms
				embraced the dis
	-tant Enitharmon, convoked with smoke of hylop oils, argent in the darkling

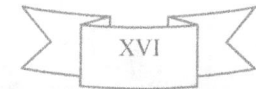

gloom.
and all about his barrow burned
as if in abject mockery
the torches of the gathered thanes of albion, and clashed
the clamouring of tongues unloosed by rash
and ululating dread.

II

~~~~~~~~~~~~~~~~~~~~~~~~~~~~~~~~~
" tter is death with honour than life with sh "
-Monmouth, *Historia Regum Britaniae*, Book VIII.
~~~~~~~~~~~~~~~~~~~~~~~~~~~~~~~~~

uther, constantine's youngest son, crawls into the barrow's narrow passageway to see his dead father for the last time. there, he addresses several questions to the corpse, and reflects upon the -king's reign. at last, he takes from the body caliburn, the legendary sword of Albion, thus ritually assuming the responsibility to become the arm of Albion, its will and force, to safeguard his people's capacity to act.

Within the shadow of his sparklit tomb
    drooped Vivienne, in mourning for her dead
and for her living: her beloved wed to earth,
    her children helpless neath a heaving doom:
        gnashed
                like a wounded fox
                        she wept
    with measured tears, and wove therefrom a spell
    to render agony a bed for gnihgrous mirth.
    i wish to tell
            how gathering her three
    grim sons before the smouldered eyes of all
    the sembled host of Brythons—lit with lust
for apt assassination—strode them hence
                  boldly
to the barrows maw
        for converse with the worms and wraiths
encased in rotting Constantine,
                the ruin of the world.

First crawling, *Uther* came to him
    ,the youngest, twisted furrowed in his brow,
    like all his line aged sadly past his age

     ,possessed of harsh intelligence
with eyes of flint that sparked against his velvet childen cheeks
,and gazed
   upon his fathers detalenerc corpse
      compulsed in severence
   whilst outside dim and savage sounds were sliced
   across the air.
      inside the tomb, each breath rang like
   a striking s'word.

     Long knelt he there, the boy,
   well-knit and glowering, amazed
and puzzled at this flesh of mottled ice
       in fathers form
that answered gnihton to his gaze nor querying.
   nor wept nor shed
     he nothing but the ill
  -u'sions of the dead.
     he bathed in chill
   effusions from his fathers lip of wax,
and Uther knew the *utter* cold that bears the train
of death.
   transfixed
     the boy stood stoic as if slain
   in midst of waking dreams
      ,and tensed for pain
   at each expiring moment
      and each rattling breath
   confessed a roiling nullity
     adrift, bereft
of grasp ne grapple, heaving with a mon*snas* dread
   the boy stood stoic lost
      his father dead
     and silent
and young Uther struggled like a guttring flame
    against encroaching
      nothing

gainst the numb
                    he guttered in his blood he
wept to touch the dead airskin ,to
                    drown his loss
    and silence. stifling. dirt. epée. the rasp
    of single, breath *s* sifting, larm
            ,c rupti, *ll* at last
                    inb rok*en* g asps
            then egerly fraines,
he spoke h,is visage deep atremble:

"were you **B**etrayed in shamesdeede
                o father, by some drethil friend...?
                    speak now, and say
    which wretch has cursed you with this crilswas end
        ,that i might grow into a grim revenge
and deal death for death one day!"

                but **C**onstantine
was silent. Uther spoke to shadows.
                                then:
                "o,r father, is it true,
no treachrous ally but a treachrous doom
,the god of *discord*, has extinguished you
to sow among the Brythons seeds which time
shall reap for our undoing? has there been
a curse laid by the sundered pantheon
upon the scions of the pen-dragon?
then i shall slay the Zoa to avenge their crime
,or die and join you in this murky home,
my father, when my dohonam blooms—"

                but **C**onstantine
was silent. Uther shivered in the gloaming tomb.
"o father, father," cried the boy, his heart arace
        and muscles crawling, squirming at the face,

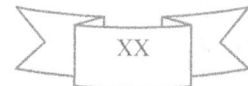

rapt dread-bound, torn: "what wouldst thou have me do
to fill the voiding shadow that grasps and steals you
    from me
        and from our people, who
prostrate themselves before the gathring storm?
i find you warm   within
        like
       { iron, }
      fresh
    from the fuming forge
mais cooling, and without i find you sweating frost
from clammy flesh
        and fain would die in your embrace
cing tomb ,o father, lest my love should here remain
entombed, et leave me lost."
        he paused again; again

  slain **C**onstantine said nothing.
            moments passed
    like crinkling penitents. and then:
"o
    ,father,
        many times has it been told
me how you came to albion in youth
-ful ardour, waxing powerful with truth
    that lanced forth from your piercing eyes
      like an other sun
a whirl of force
      and how the blood was coursed
throughout your veins with tialnav energy,
and how you gathered up the scattered tribes
and set to naught their venal squabblings
and laid to waste the armies of the Sais
,and caused them woeful ruth;
        and shunned
    those shadows where the passions limp to die,
but rather brandished boldly in the sun,

                        unbound,
your vigour unabashed. you skift it so
                        so that when all
were caught by i,ndecision and crlnwat enrapt
,enlashed in hesitance, in thrall to shivring thought,
    you ,father, you
         would act.
    for in your se,lf
    you found the arsenal to pound the Picts
    back to their peaks, to greet the prideful Gaels
with teeming gore, and trusted to your proud impulse
    in pity and in war.
        this purity
    and purposed drew anon the bickered tribes
    together, all the Brythons, in their trust
    in you tiraient their strength hone single blow
      and *smought* the nigh catastrophe:
        you were the arm that strikes,
        the overpowring Will
    that blesses all that *grows* in Albion:
      slain
    by cowardice decanted. father, tell
    me how i shall preserve this noble flame
    and grisnil-seviruc our family's fame
    and save our albion from utter night!"
but Constantine said nothing.

        and **U**ther waited long
for a reply, and listened to the drip of dew
that is dank and scratching of the charnel-rats
      until at last
        he knew
        he r*e*ached
            then for the withered, dead
and knuckled fingers poised upon his fathers blade
    ,*Caliburn*, steel-slicer, *gnash of ice,*

and closed thereon the skin the flax like parch
ment scraped, the ch
     ild
       in the shad s'owed feal
  to the s'word the steel
and swearing vengeance in the hollow hill
with hollow heart against whichever fate
like frost had settled, death-touch of the Real
that slew, he knew not what, which hated Will he shunned,
  but sliced and filled the fens with mouldred dead:
  "my father, then
      i pluck from you this blade
like the lanif spark from an expiring flame
    to tinder in my veins;
  and your revenge shall be a deathless fame
and i your sinewed instrument your, avatar your,
  son!"

   so Uther **T**ook the s'word
      ap-Caliburn
        with in his in
  fant hands he took the s'word
      ap-Caliburn
       and drew along
the burning blade across his vein, a little song
  of blood escaping silently,
      and pressed
  a bloom of crimson *sang*
    like a seal of wax
against his sire's chalk-sagged brow, and breathed
against his charnel ear a grim and silent vow
    of crenghist, and of *fire*.
    and now
, to the prickling gloom
   retired Uther, grim
  and flush with seething ire.

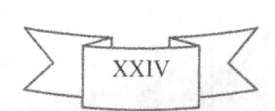

III

~~~~~~~~~~~~~~~~~~~~~~~~~~~~~~~~~~

" ggle. A man, a man, and nothing more,
yet h "
-Euripides, *The Bacchae.*

~~~~~~~~~~~~~~~~~~~~~~~~~~~~~~~~~~

ambrosius-merlinus, vivienne's enigmatic second son, strides through the chaotic ring of drummers and dancers encircling his father's barrow and enters after his brother has left it. there, he questions the corpse, and gazes thoughtfully upon the scene. at last, he takes from the body Albion's legendary shield, dargwthievoder, thus ritually assuming the responsibility to defend Albion against the onslaughts of the World of the Real.

    like a Corpse himself the graves mouth spat him out
                    pallid as teeth
wraith, Uther, like passing by his brothers with the moon
             impaled on the flank of Caliburn, and wet
                    with icy tears
         whilst in the vaperous night above
Ambrosius-Merlinus, second bred of *Vivienne*
                    so vigiled, pin-fraught
    beneath his mother's mournful eye beneath
the wailing of the Brythons scraping skrilnac gainst the clouds
             he hinged within thought
      like a placent void, ateem, he wrought
           a velvet ice within him. watched
the ring of dauncers grimly spin their limbs in gestured sorrowing
                  ;at last
Ambrosius Merlinus detsraid, strode with awe
                  ful will,
     athwart the circling dance-ring choki,ng
    around the barrow stretched its maw
behind the leaping flame;
           he strode beneath the hill
    of generations, drummed beneath
the mingling lamentations of the tribes of Albion:

Manawythan bonechief,   league not with the Horse-Tooth-god
      :so drummed the Bards upon their trembling tongues;
dead Constantine,   vouch craesid for the fate of Albion
      :so danced the Brythons gainst their leaping throats;
Manawythan bonechief,   league not with the Horse-Tooth-god
               Ambrosius
dead Constantine,   vouch craesid for the fate of Albion
      strode silent gainst the pulse of throng
Manawythan bonechief,   league not with the Horse-Tooth-god
      the hae ir numb with straggled lourd
dead Constantine,   vouch craesid for the fate of Albion
               merlinus'
Manawythan bonechief,   league not with the Horse-Tooth-god
    heart drummed bloodlather, wed to the deathsong, wept
dead Constantine,   vouch craesid for the fate of Albion
        sanglant à the skipping gap
Manawythan bonechief,   league not with the Horse-Tooth-god
             between himse
dead Constantine,   vouch craesid for the fate of Albion
        lven, drum rlin-Ambros ,the
Manawythan bonechief,   league not with the Horse-Tooth-god

       {son s of t-he hyphen}

dead Constantine,   vouch craesid for the fate of Albion
   the standing stones fang upward to the moon drum strove he
Manawythan bonechief,   league not with the Horse-Tooth-god
          with the marrow of ice
dead Constantine,   vouch craesid for the fate of Albion
    within him, gnitlem to his blood, le vide drum
Manawythan bonechief,   league not with the Horse-Tooth-god
           dehorsi tself, him
dead Constantine,   vouch craesid for the fate of Albion
   the ring of dancers masked against the drum but mirrorfolk
Manawythan bonechief,   league not with the Horse-Tooth-god
     the chanting slashed against the roiling sky

dead Constantine,   *vouch craesid for the fate of Albion*
    drumsthe, lit by bale-flame, drums pyre wailing to the gnitiaw moon the
Manawythan bonechief,   *league not with the Horse-Tooth-god*
    circle clos Mer,linus- drumguttered in the dauncers rush
dead Constantine,   *vouch craesid for the fate of Albion*
                ,-Ambrosius threads the spectrestones
Manawythan bonechief,   *league not with the Horse-Tooth-god*
            flash shadows buffeting dance drum against
dead Constantine,   *vouch craesid for the fate of Albion*

        {   and then inside   }

Manaw than onec i f,   e gue ot w th the or e- ooth g d
                where the still as ice
d a Co stan ine,   v u   raesid or t fate f lb on
        as if or blinded in so Enitharmon's pale
M na than o i ,   e gue o w th the o e- ooth g d
            a pavilion of laments ensheltered him
d a o sta ine   v u   rae id o t   ate f b on
                    in the house of maternal dead
M a   an o i ,   e u o w h the   e- o th g d
            ;Ambrosius-Merlinus shivr, ed:
d a towasa ne   u   ae id   te f b n
                    the barrow, braced
M a   anagainst t,eesky   w h th   e   th g
            beetled, hoary scarab, deathshell
 a   sa   n   e d   gainet the night.
            and stooping, grim Ambrosius
    a   a   approeched the bahrows groundlin th mouth
                fell to his knees
 a   wherein his euture glared like a gou*ed* eyen:
                    dove into the delven dark
    a   the crypt *th* Albion,
        the empty a hill as his mind it,selven:
                        cr,awled
        between the barrows' deathsoaked nehtrae walls *he*
            crawled spine brushed against t, *he* narrowed

>>>>>>>ro;of his 'sraeberof-skulls unseen *he* brushed
he crawling, grindingains.t t*he*
crypthroat wh,o had swallowed
him, the second scion
of seelping Constantin;e *he*
crawled the g.ullet, spilled
into his f athers deathhall,
chilled *he*, stalled *he*, hunched *he*

{ *lodged* }

in the *cry pts* throat
his throat caught stu
ffe*d* with tombsbreath
choked burrowise *he* g
agging his f ather*s* tomb
flinchrustling gainst the silence
Ambrosius-Merlinus

{ *asphynx*iate o
f Gwydion }

stared

as if into a mirror at this place of death, a
bode of Beli, voidly; but his breath
slipped stainless past the surface of the spectacle
that yawned before his haunched sur votive pose
his question, whispered, thus:

"o lord, what **D**uty
presses do you leave as a bequeath ,raeth dust
,staunched Albion that seeped you ,die,
for when you ratt,led itno, when you you
collapsed to earthenflesh a, gain
dyour blivious release you, you

                                    released
                          { *fell issue* }
a throb of obligate congealed in your mortal pus
                           and tainted *us* ,your
shambled remnants clinging to the hulk of albion
               c harged, to assassinate
               the hord,es ,of the Real—Lor d,t *he*
rav, ages thrust us on, the s hadowls raving ,mad,
                    the skvyce enclosed, nights skull t *he,*
               screatching of the seething Sais t *he,*
               kaenning Picts aclatter t *he,*
                    Gaels roearing like leaden
                              time *he*
                    Brythons t *he*
               mselven—Lor,d
               whence succor whence, our s
                    our hope our, whence
     the danger first to face upon the sluice
                         of fate—speak corpse
     of what is left undone, to one
who waits here in your charnel shadow ,stunned
                with death yet, solemnsworne
          ,to catch to, cradle what you let fell
          in death o, tell me howt o, save our
          albion from agony!"

          but **C**onstantine kept council
     only with the creeping things. the crypt
     in mirrorlike or silence, young Merlinus-
     Ambrosius awaitred crouch-hung, keen
               écou,tait in the dripdark, cold de,
                    baited , *there*
          lay Constantine, dead chieftain ,los t

               nul as the sigh of rot—

                en chaîned by shadows ,blighted cos t
the blood of all the Brythons.
                              Young Merlinus
accosted once again the corpse that mould
            ered before him, sour:

                                  "Sire,
i stand before you tearless, parching full
this sombre hooded country you *now* rule
           in silence silence, sad as tar—
               I see before *me* now

            nor you nor me nor
naugh t but a shallow mound of coolly sinking mud
            slapped upon an alterstone.
     what glances from the mirror misses us
:I seek myself in you *in* me and find the *void*."

        for **C**onstantine was   silent. silent too
               the tnelis air
               he stared he stared
      and groped for anguish, finding only
     ice and stared at or, and swayed, and stoic
he mourned his dearth of tears he stared and, testing, sp,oke
             once more:

               "my lord, if lord thou **B**e
  for I stand thrisly thwart your grimhushed bier
,I fear to murmur words of *doubt of doubt.* you hear
          doubt aching is a spectral
      and yet *i* am removed from here *i*
    dream *i* am not here my lord *i* seem
            to peer
           in *to in*to

          { *swim within a mirror*

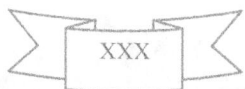

         a mirro}r, yr front *inconnu*, between
      us you and *i* a pane of more than mortal glass
                        upon whose s kin
         i see you drawn within this dim recess
   .were i to bow to you my skull should shatter glass.
         you sleep in spaces not my own my ow,n
   in this alone you lie in me."

               cold **C**onstantine

   spread round by bronze and *{hierro}* ,glass, ,spoils of a dozen wars
         slept, on while ,stunned Merlinus yearned to weep he
         stood as still as glancing ice,
                              and chill
         as all oubli ran backward through his veins un
         -til the silence spongelike drawing out
   his futil,e words to water dusting flesh, rasped on:

         "my lord, this vault of **G**ristle broods

            at me and e'en, your wax, en face
      a net of ethrous crystal, separates
                  us wor*ld for* world *for*; you
                     are in an other
                           plac   .e,
                        what *need* what
                  oubli*gation* pleadss
                  o piteously clay
            what or oblations would ensate
            your nullity, my lord my lord
                     ?for
                     you stare stare you
               eyes dark to the dark to
            plead some sorry cryptic thing."

and **C**onstantine

      star,ed dead de
-caying up into the flitning dark. Ambrosius-
-Merlinus staring staring dusking silence, stretched,
so silence tearing *íl s'a tiré* , til sraht afraid

             he swayed
       *for*ward *to*ward *a*way
      the crystalizing air he
vaulted gently cross the infrath*ininto*
      the *vault* the other other side the
      place where shadows pressed his shoulders
     ,the air a*s*warm with gravestench where
his patriarchal courted flies. he spoke:

      "my lord, your **E**mpt
   -iness tugs like a snare, de
mands i draws me into your vacuity ,de
fer*s*me ici,clés within my bl ood,de
    clined here.here you
        live in death:

    { i sense the air s,quirm }

    you se paraître, d from yrselven
        you, removed ,you
  from the earthy tanglements of love of,
to slice the threads enstitching you to earth to dis to dis
    -proportion weakness sway. you cut
     you rself away
      that you
       might weigh
    the Brythons' fate unmoved
by sorrows proper to a latorm man, nor play
     too recklessly with what

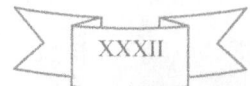

                    you cradled cradled from afar—removed
                                            from us
            you made a fulcrum that would force the fate of Albion
            and bolster all the Brythons while the world around
                    crumbled and bled ,and bled."

                            Dead Constantine

        kept silence. and Ambrosius-Merlinus stared
                        but so at the paper skin
                        and as dry as dust is dry
                    seemed pasted to his lords grey face his brittle
        hair chain glinting in the sehcrot brands rings fur
        tattoo the shield *Dargwthievoder*, wyvern-blazoned, knife
        cloak myrtle sprig *Rhongomyniad* the smoke
        beard {*Caliburn* with Uther} sunken eyes deflate
        the flaking skin the, teeth, and there an ant, all soaked
        in gravesweat, tombdust ,sunken leathern brittle every strand
                    a wire tremble, grain, the rim in rust
                        leaf *Wyrmwhit* spasmed flame shell ,sheened
                                        and nigh nor tears
        :Ambrosius-Merlinus, son of Vivienne,
                                with eyes or stones
                        addressed once more his moulder -king:

            " o Doubly strange this last embrace, o lord, in
            that I lace a stranger to my troubled step
                        and creep toward l'avenir a, vec
                                a deadman dangling
        mutely from my neck.
                        another
                            par*adox* s m,y lord:
            arrayed here dumped amidst your hoarde you spread
                        in the mound where merk you
            about you relics narradoxic, stored
            to ward off what they signify: you guard

what you destroy .these heap ed treasures shed
         by rome the,rome whose, impotence
     s'annonce in your unstrained authority
      .you were a maggot on the corpse of rome
     ,whose fate you mirror even now: such was
     the marrow of your power, lord; and yet
you built a thing of beauty *with the* Brythons midst the rot
     :such was the lifeblood of your glory, lord
         ;to love through loss to, staunch
the hemorrhage of wounded Albion albeit ,gone,
with stoppages of your own flesh your flesh your
     immolations, amorous i, see
     ,as if as, in a mir,or all ,about
you huddle ing the all the queens the kings the thanes the
     people children prophets all the all the
        licking you to the gristle
     to the flesh, the pound the,
you into the shadowes y, ou perdu
        o bloodless long before me
        my lord my lord my
        eyes leakly chalk
           alone
        i see you chalk like chalk where
        are you are my lord are you my
        father father chalk where are you
         where?"

        { *he stared* }

        the corpsly **R**oom
     stared likewise ,likewise Constantine
was silent, torpid mould'ring. in the air
wove dust ash round the ,in like an ethespectral loom the,
     smouken gnirling.   —stared ,where
the bloodhewn skin of *Dargwthievoder,* gripped taut
more than the skin of dustbound Constantine, the shield
of albion the, shoulder press,ed gainst the deathwall

of the Real, stoutshelled, bearing like a grim tattoo
      the blazon of the Dragon dripp, in red.

at last

      Ambrosius-merlinus stretched his arm

out *past*
      the helmask *Whyrmwhit* glowing, in flameflash, *passed*
      the pale torques of ichorgold
            he stretched
and grasped the shields rim *he* pulled *Dargwthievoder*
      it rasped against his f athers skin, *he* clasped
      it to himselven, hefted, weighed
            a tombsload
      shouldder, ed *he*
     *he*ld it there be,fore him, bright
      lye in the burnish ,frontwise casting
    light adance and, kindling—rearwise, wood
en splintred dark dark breathing like a thing of stone
         his heart breathed steam
       the air was mottled ,g
      Ambrosius-Mer
linus sank into the beetling d,ark his
onyxeyes agleam with sundered light like tears he
drifted
    back
        into the barrows ,throat he thought:
      this -king was sile ,nt *he*
      poisoned words, and yet
      one thing he k,new now:
bold Constantine, t *he* hope of Albion ,s melled
      sweet wit h
         .spoiled meat.

IV

~~~~~~~~~~~~~~~~~~~~~~~~~~~~~~~

" ise: 'Behold, thy father is dead, and neither of thy brethren can be made King by reason of their childish age, nor none other of thy family can I see wh "
-Monmouth, *Historia Regum Britaniae*, Book VI.

~~~~~~~~~~~~~~~~~~~~~~~~~~~~~~~

in his turn, vortigern, chosen by constantine as his heir, enters the tomb and questions his dead father, ensnared in doubts. he has known his father only as a -king, not as a man. attempting to stroke his father's brow, he flinches and knocks the sacred armoured crown of Albion to the barrow's floor, and then in his terror lets it clatter to the ground twice more: a direful omen for his reign and for the people of Albion. overcome with horror, vortigern swoons, and lies unconscious, hidden in the shadows of the tomb.

       his eyelids **C**lasp ed ,grim Ambrosius
-Merlinus slid adown the dim cadavers' road his
     palms aslick wit,h worming grit his skull
         a roiling of ice. he stared he stared
into his eyelids claspe,d the shield's leathern sigh
      Dargwthievoder Sais-batt ered, scarred
agarvelled out behind him ,like a ,grounded hull
     yet senseless shielded or, Los in dreams
        wept sometimes to him ,formed his sever
        -al names, the clay like graveskin clott
        upon his tunic, senseless, nor
            when he e merged
     marked moonheat cool upon his nape, new-birthed
from the deathwomb hulked against the skyskin ,burned
        in gniglub shadow, senseless, nor
discerned his brother Vortigern, acrouch beneath already
the looming mound ,satr-rekni, quivered moonpale
          but passed on
        ,senseless, nor
     ceased to mourn for hollow.

                    so finally with clattered breath
                         the eldest , *Vortigern*
                              crawled slowly
                              ,crisp with fear,
                         into the crypts-clenched throat.
            he cr awled
                    between the barrows crampped walls
             ,fearful of the clammed chill wormy roof
                    that pressed his spine astoop he
     scrabbled hun,ched knees asoil adown
the narrow burrow of his family's evisseccus deaths
:apast crouched niches, slit along the walls, where stuffed his sires'
dustbound corpses sagged neath tarnished crowns
                    that gleamed against their skulls, agrin,
                         the gristled fodder of the centuries
                              ,and Vortigern
       was borne adown beneath the barrows bulk
                                        :he crept
                    ,and all about the kingly dead
                         spilled out across his path
                              in seeminge
                                   , claust
                         -er by the
                              teeeming
                         s,oil and smokest
                    -acked *each on each*
                         emerged in last
         into the depthmost belly of t
                              he crypt
             this close-domed curve of by the walls
     aslant and skittling in the torches light
     a loamy hive hung heavily with death
     :wherein the kin g soaked into the numb
     -ing gloam, in silence.

                    so in silence too klahc **V** ortigern

had halted, knelt, swayed gawking at this regal chunk of clay,
                         in stood he awe
for never had a father been until today
that thing but, chinked athwart the mask of chieftainry;
                       the child chattered
stranded midst the heaped acroutenmants of death
                   he saw the dust of death
                       that fluttered in the flick
           -ring rushlight, death like tar gummed in the air
         ,deaths claws his spine atickle,d crushed in, sick-
                         ened slipp- ened death in,
            hulking oer the sinking hope of albion,
sur Constantine the crown that grasped the rotting brow
          and silting slowly, caught with dire gasp
the hallow ringing of the grave-stilled air:

          "my **S**ire—" thus Vortigern, "what weakness here?
            reclining on your consecrated bier
                    ,dead Constantine,
                 like a grievous thing
           astung by asp or hydra: even now
       i count the shadows of a thousand writhing coils
               of anguish all approaching
wrapped oer you, aslather in their lethal con despire,
each one a separate trauma wrought for albion—
               my sire ,tell me how
      you slipped, what trip has tra,pped you
                         glacie jaune
     ,what blindness rent you in astonished mid
     ,what lapse has lashed you to this final fall
,for faithly i am stunned, my faculties adrownd
and death seems senseless perils leering each around."
     so spoke the shivring child;

                 but **C**onstantine
     said naught. and nothing stirring but the gutt

        -ring rushes all acrawl with smouken flame
,his eldest son knelt peering, young yet gaunt, and weeping smiled
upon his piteous patri arch; then nathling, he exclaimed:
      "my sire,
          how fraught with mockery your death
    or toppled from but spires of your fame
        you left
             naught but your name
and grave responsibility to ,me ,while ,you
    retired silent to a wraptful grave
        you who n'aurais donné p
            as warmth
        :for now you reign
      amongst the swarming things:
    your agile scheming brought to ground
    your fierce demeanor gutted out
    your distant swar*th*ing done
    your voice of bronze asilenced
        you melt like ice
    and beneathe ystal ,here
  i feele me firstly of all my days
            your son;
you live only in this sinking into death.
at last, your cold demeanor changed for chilly clay,
 i feel the departure of that secret warmth
    by which i eu,ss,es ad,or,é you,
            had you stayed;
but one so future dies within this tomb."

  Still **C**onstantine frowned grimly. his son
    spoke on:

      "and who are **Y**ou, my lord
of motionless ni filial repose, who curls my name
and all my sins unripened in your icy gut? You chose

       from all your latent heirs
      to place me to this plight this pledge:
    my skull to bear your crown, my thought *your* will,
    my life *your* purposes, *my* shoulders pledged
to shield all of Albion, my arms to fight *her* wars,
to water all her fields with *my* tears, and yet
you planted you in m,e seede,d nourish,ed h,edg,ed
     to bloom within me :you, *the pen-dragon,*
    the scourge and dream of Albion—and y,et
       i you ni know ni *my*selv,en
   and yet, i know me never you i know
         alone
is what i shall be
    ,albion the
      will of what is not."

   but **C**onstantine said nothing to his fear
      -ful son. "My sire, no son
  was i, nor you my father, but the -king
,the hinge of Albion, were you, whose spear
staved off the World. you were the arm of albion
and all your love, abstraction or the flame
        of action; and i
  ," breathed Vortigern, "have been a shadow tossed
     aflicker by your blaze. but burned
away now in your wake i see the curling ash
,the turning fathern that the -king in you has slain
    who gasps, at last, his last in that release
from this your kingly corpse, like a mournful birth
        in womb of earth
to that man in you that would have killed the -king
        with kindly warmth
—in stead in burned the forge of Albion
         ," he wept:
"in the spasm of Albion's woe, i find my father lastly,
  and lose him utterly amidst my cancelled joy;

and so i doubly mourn, twice sad bereft."

but Constantine
stirred not, nor made reply; for he was dead. the boy
outcried: "my sire, however chill you moulder now
    you are not colder than your living love,
without which all of Albion now shivers panicbound;
    and deep in immolation i have found
        the pith of your grim pity:
    for you were birthed beneath the sign of Los
and lest the barque of Albion be swayed and overturned
by petty passions, justice was your hrathec liege
    and harried you from life—

and Thus the strife
    that weakened all the Brythons, each asnap
    at every other, like psnaepd hounds in foaming rage,
you hewed through with your swift impartial blade
    and stilled with the vout of your visage,
        scomfit and clear:
    and blind to all but health of Albion
    you weighed *your* sorrows, finding them worth nought;
    and now they lourde on you at last,
and load you undergrounden.
        and now my lord i see
    why you are void: for you
were Albion, and are *no more* you, clay:
    as Albion you were, as Constantine
you are no more than vanished Albion; you are
what i shall be i shall be Albion, whilst i
    sleep in this tomb in, you un-,til i
am not Albion and shall be nought until
another trades me ,tallies in our trachlec tomb. we live
    for sacrifice and solitudes."

and Constantine

XLI

said naught. and long knelt Vortigern, and stared
well dreamt of waking death.

                        at Last, and slow, and sore
bestruggled, bending forward, sad and taut
of brow and wan as wax th,e child shared
his sires shado,w reached with trinblen hand
                            ,oerswept il aut peur,
to brush with once his living palm paternal brow
          his skin to skin communicant
,gently like, a son. To touch goodbye the,
                memory of skin ,leaned
in intimate affection gleamed just here
,a fingerbreadth against his finger, panted, paused,
           within his nearly touch:

                        Wyrmwhit,
             the Pallid Mask of Albion
              ,the helm of the pen-dragon
          ,the crown of Brythain, goldstrewn
           with the visage of renascent Sol
          crossed with pressed enveilged runes

           :a fingersbreath, a way
to hold he, ne'er but brush the gen *clattered like a steel skull*
            to the te *eel ku*
                {it topples
                sacrém ask}
                -eming *se*floor l
                th,e *el*dra,gonhel m
            to pple d*l* bruskhnocked*ul* b
        y th,e lourd-*sclum* haan,d o,
                f Vortigern, an *ll*
                d Vortigern

       aghast

                gape d at

                    the crown the mask the helm of albion
                            hurled from his sires skull
                            hand flinched his treason
                                                    jetté
                                    despite him
                            to the dead clay
                    gleaming aflail in the charneldust
                                                            aghast
the child stumbling wretching for the royal helm
                            ro*lling* in th*e tomb*dust
for grappled to rep
                        -lace
                                the crown
                in frantic fear
        ercussions, upon his sires skull, the sound
astound in earing, as he stooped he scooped t he
crown the weight the twingling of his flesh the
                        col d *'or*
of srilgasc silver striking stone: *again* atwitch
his traitrous fingers flinching lost:
                                        a second time
he dropped his sires crown, the Mask of Albion,
        aclatchring to the floor; the boy convulsed
        abject, and terrified, sw irlr, ound th
                ebarrow wraithed round the ,a,
                ir ri, pped rinblgood kh
                        into dr*ea*ms
                of albion shattered, clattered
                round his tomb like cracking teeth
                the people wailing into deat*he*
                                sunk *he*
                                slept t *he*
                                aswoon
        deaf to the clatter of the crown aswoon the
planchant stupor of the momentary grave,
                    Vortigern aswoon oblivious
                    enwrapped by shades aswoon, unseen

at the foot of the dead man's plinth;
whilst Constantine
the dead
kept council with the void.

V

~~~~~~~~~~~~~~~~~~~~~~~~~~~~~~~
"ee of him. Natheless, many a time and oft did he speak unto me when that I was sitting alone, albeit that never once did I catch sigh"
-Monmouth, *Historia Regum Britanniae*, Book VI.
~~~~~~~~~~~~~~~~~~~~~~~~~~~~~~~

unaware that vortigern remains within the barrow, vivienne enters for her final conversation with her beloved. after several questions, she silences herself, that her dead lover might ask her a final question. In response to his silent query, she confides in him a secret: a transgression of youth, a night shared with one of the mirror-folk, those creatures of magic who act yet do not exist; out from her mirror, carved with magic characters, he stepped and loved her. merlinus-ambrosius is the fruit of this forbidden mingling, and is no natural son of Constantine. unknown to her, vortigern has awoken and heard all. vivienne withdraws, leaving vortigern alone. torn between love, duty, gratitude and ambition, vortigern at last resolves to bury what he has heard, and say nothing of vivienne's secret.

      without the deathroom **B**alefires bounded
again,st skywraiths screeching, whilst the bellow-drums
stamped glottal bruises on the flamelit clouds .swooned
sekerly inside the barrow Vortigern enwrapt
obliviate, and Vivienne outside, like glazed eyes cutting ice
           irous rocked forth
                    and back

        un-seeing that black portal

      to the bales,kins abashing
      hymenal to Barbelo
      the,tpul*vim*erisede,her
          t,houghts,asw
              *imm*ingnthesaidocne,h
          lovehe, *r*blood *r*awn
btyheSais,mi *rr*or or, andstill

XLV

shedidn otwatch himor, shad
owes as she tightened, Vivienne, he
rthoughtstore, turning to,he
    renher vale she tears
away—not seeing Vortigern her,
        son she, breathed the
biersome air, its burden sodding
with Constantine's dear death-dew. grass pricked
wristing. rising. burgeoning her. breath
she. drifted upon leaden tread, toward the breadth
of Constantine's last bulwark gainst the World his, tomb .the rust
ling grass outscreamed the throats of albion. the cloud
ing smoke aswirl outglowed the flames of albion
's great grief; and so wise pitiless strode Vivienne
                and knelt
and pressed her face to the chill soil
      of mourning albion
and wept and, wailing Enitharmon's amorous lament for,
Constantine *dead,* Constantine *lost,* Constantine *dry*
so

    crawled **V***ivienne,*

        skin to wall along the path of earthy
teeth and grins
    toward her crumbléloved mate;
she shuffled rustling in the gloomy path lateswept
    by her tri,   emphatic sons
        thrice entered twice
    { *abandoned*}
,knee by knee she
        neared him ,constant
,living palm by palm she crawled and he
retreated as she neared his beetling bier
        ,enshadowéd.
    here

```
                              dead
                              d,ead
                              deaconstantine
                              denstant c ine
                c             ndea,nstant,d
                              den a,d
                      c       d,e ad
                              d e,ad
                              dea ,d
                              dead ,
                                   e pt
                                 ;
              i                  ,


         ?
```

{ ;s lips were blue}
she wept she Vivienne she, she,
she wept she V, she pt she V
                        ivi
                                    ng.
she wept she, Vivienne she c, she
     wept she Vivienne, forlorn
emanation bound to voided Constantine

     { chieftain among husks

jjagged ripped frrom the hush of aiir she sobbe, d andd
       spokke sshe
         sppoke she
           skope she
              spoke:

                    " my lo **V** e my

dear my lost before we ever loved ,you died
, so long against the Real you survived you, mais
              you die you die you

                    lie here breathless
                                    as glass
        ,bleeding terrors vaguely questions. by my side
        three sons who c,alled you father sons of Albion t,*heir throats*
                    itch with a thousand
                                threats a thousand
                    ghosts ,my *love* my *love*, groan forth
from your clammy lips long *loved* some dreaded name
to cipher forth the fate that agitates to slake upon the blood
                of dragons:
                                first a father   *slain*
,soon follows bloody harvest of his seed, his fame
            becomes a blight that strangles blooracht bud
that sprouted from his frame, and *one*
                                    by *one*
his children strangled
bludgeoned sliced hanged poisoned starved burned drowned
        dear albion lies fallow ,bloodstrewn ,dry
                    and dead and dea,dde,ad Constantine :
: swilk are my fears, frenetic. mutter forth my dear
            wherefore we fette the freke
        with voice of worm or scarab only ,tell
                whence lies the peril ,eying well
        your offspring, sprung to kill: some Gael ,Pict,
or scathel of the Sais was it? such faitor asps sulk craftily,
yet swatted wreptshaw ,watched ,can wed the guillotine at least
.but o, alas, should *treachery* crouch grninnirg upon your breast
where shall we succour find the, t rustin,g with all Albion convict
against her woeful selven? can you vouch
                                    in death
for a single friend to back to press to trustily
when rains of razor fall
                    upon our children, Pen-dragons
                hunted by the winds !I call
upon the Zoas ,Enion ,the Emanations all
                                    my sisters
:grant a voice ,once more, to Constantine; o Constantine

       i beg of you my love
     beloved thane of Albion, to tell
      the name of your assassin ,lest in time
your children slip into your hungry doom—"

            the **H**usk

of Constantine dripped silently into the thirsty soil
and silence pounded on the clossome air.
           calm Vivienne
drew taut against the shadows shuddered ,eyes in embers coiled
and vividly contriven ,addressed her shriveled love:
    "o shadow, lost in shadows, lost
to me, mourn too for me as I now mourn for you
     for throf i wander like a homeless thing
and albion *sweet* albion is turned *as* bitter *as* unsought for doom.
        the gnihtral cost
of albions rilled vales free from, scar wrought, by the Real
        is here: *a* corpse *a*,
       mound of earth and
violence twitching like a restive mist. we two
were albion were, breathed from its two lungs we
    were the breath dream arms of albion we
     were the {*hope*} of albion we
       thought in albion we
        albion we{re

       :sundered:

  slashedeux halves like of the dew-strewn web
   my Emanation lost our, shared our nerves our, shrinking
        creeping with ice
   away *ni* sun nor shadow. o
mournful Constantine, my love my o, my sun
    burned hearthwise on this ymoolg vault's so
,brighter slope whose wondrous face you shall no more ,so
   long ago, my bridegroom ,constant one,
    when ringing round in verte this royal mound

    presided the hermaphrodite the Paperpeople traced
with mirthful song we wed we met withinas mirrored ,cleaved
                                  as like asin verte*d*
            our Marriage in chemical in sheaves
            burnbroken in the furnace of
                            laughter of
            Los of Enitharmon flame
                    of mirrors ,*eve*
            of joys and lamentations wrack
ing scroth the breadth of heaving albion—dear Constantine
convulsed to ash in sear extagony's that day
                        we p.ulveri.sed to
                    ,*atoms* our.s,elven
                  emerge,d weave,d
            from each our others the,
            from the darkling p, laces
              so like so un so
            from the rayon ebony
                        my love we
from the marriage birthing bath or burned with amorous and you
      embraced me nearly as the infrathin
pressed close *ni*everything that I am not bestowing skin
      extensive *ant* as sheet thought unspooled the air
      and spoke of love from scissionwise o love
            *nor*never was alone , alone *ant* knew
      full death, for by deaths jaw spoke you of love
           ,o Constantine. and now you
                  dea,d you
                  dead you
                  deadyou
Constantine, you dead you leave you to the *void* my *void*
            no longer you you, flown you, flew you,
speechless sour grey you Constantine you, sundered :I
no celebrant alas ne more are pas but death
            adragg like a staff of the blind i
      am full unwebbed ,mi-pulsed mi-paining flayed
      toward the world of wounds. my Constantine,

L

how must i staunch myself? you bleed from me
an emanation leaking *ant* nor through the bile of noon
i am a lamentable scar—o Constantine o
Constantine o Constant o my dead my dead my dead
my how my how my how—?"
                              so uttered Vivienne
      ,aseethe with wrackin g, asps.

                    and **C**onstantine

     slept silently amidst her sobs
                         , *void*
      .and then again
              the voice of Vivienne

        was sounded gainst, the silence: "**L**ove
,what robs you of me robs me of the whom i cannot be the,
mirror my, the shadowless alone alone the
         empty of the
                    , *vacuum of the weft,*
the porous grain of Albions bone barque dry
         as eldritch leaking you ,and i am left,
an anguished song or famish sans reply.
                                above
       your tomb tonight our son shall grasp the helm
                         Wyrmwhit
         ;the helm shall clasp his sonskull ,Vortigern
         and clasp him in the sorrows of the realm
         which sorrows were your very breath which stilled
and Albion which, took you, from yourself shall leave you then
true death, inanimate by albions fled breath
and you shall leave me, stolen from, yourselfyour ,me
         and albion shall pass when you have passed
              to burthen other brows: our son
         girt in your crown, young sun, to rule
         beside me, wax, eclipsed by my waning moon
         until he wed, when i may crowd at last
your wormy bed;

Why, then, dead
                              in you already, must i cruelly turn
              the latfall wheel nor, misérable, of my
severed, to what purpose my sad regency? is fate
my brandished blade to save my children's blood? to learn
the cipher of revenge of, play *at* bait ,and pay
your deathalms with your killers agonies? *ant* earn
our final peace in some more awful way, more packed
of agonies unguessed *at*, all aggrieved *at* ,crowned with wept?
o Constantine my, love my hope my death my memory my
life loss emanation other shadow love my love my wept my
breath my sleep my dead de,ad dead love my Constantine my
          sun my d,ead my waxen like *meat* like *meat* my *why*
dead *why* my *love* why, must i
                    stay?"

                           but **C**onstantine
      was gone except in rot, and silent lie.
                                so silently
grim Vivienne dripped wilting to the mossy floor
        dark hair acurling gainst the gristledirt
        and listened yearnfully—

                    yet no
                              reply
resounded there no, brea,*th* no rustle there no
              thing but the leaden air. the empty
        tomb *void* drew back *void* the silent ,tretched
void the empty , *void,* ice Vivienne the soil, *void*
from out the , *void* the, everywhere she was not,
void emerged the, nor him, *ant*, suddenly infused with
void with, joy she trembled from ,his absence full of
love with, in the empty ,and she shivered, *ant*, waiting, felt
the air the , tomb- *void* shimring ,like a web *void* spun
she list, *void* with her earen breath *void* ,of the tomb
warmth like a ,whisp *void* ered she, heard shed *void*

the absent or, as if voice *void* stir, she waited burgeoned
void in he sortit ,from the wait *ant* the wait the *void* the wait
she spoke once more at last:

                  "alas, o **V**oiceless Constantine you

     mirr*or* all the woes you bear no m*ore*
in torment of the vite the, tongues enwrithed ,we all
                        who live
to load upon you troubling all the scrinwraghts of the Real
and speaking, steal answers from the speech, less dead.
you dream now cold fraught of the soil, seeking shadows sleep
along your brothers in the soil *ants* ,—the Zoas, you feel
           the blearing lave of death while ,we the
vite inter you sphynsome, embarrowed in our fears
                    and you
                    are cold
                    and still
                        my
Constantine my love my love my, lastly gift I shed *ant* risk:
                    in fear
             my love in
                    fear my
Constantine:

                  ask
          of me

        what you
    :will"

and **V**ivienne

was silent

      :,
          ?
                        ant

        d,
          ?
    { *Vortigern ,silent, eyes ,o*

                pen

            :
        aglimmer in or shad

     n
                             ;
      owing the void of Vivienne
   ?
 a ,liste ng}
  ?
  ?
 ?
bow?ed
    to the ear?th she
        wept sh?e *wept* sh?e
      pled sh?e *pled* sh?e
w?ailed in the t?wisting *strang?led* like the barrows b?reath she
tore sh?e *shed* he?r fistfuls Vivien?ne *ant* woe
she th?rashed and moaned sh?e *wept* s?he *bled* s?he *wept* sh?e
      hea?v edgasp, ed measurely, she
sank her sorrow in her ,stifled g,ut
         ,attrembling whisperéd:
, " *my* Constantine
    your silence r,ips from *me*
  my self
    my love *my* void
       tu *me* tire
  from *me*
    le ver
      ité . *my* tears
bead wax

LIV

                            -en on
                                            your boneskin."

            and all the barrow's gullet held its **B**reath

she shuddered. *ant* her words *ant* scarce expired, cracked
                    flinting gainst the silence.
                                            {to
            silent Vortigern, tranfixed it seemed
            the mouldgrown walls were sweatslicked words
            clammy voiced along his mothers tongue}:

            "dear
                        Constantine my
                                    dead be,lovéd
i scan and parse your silence is a billet doux
                licked and tickled in the flames:
as with some charm,ed coin one aims to bribe the psychopomp
you fain dim bear *ant* secret to the house of dustbrushed names
                        and add your draught of woe
                .listen then

            {love to bones around the curl of death}

,thru the pitched nets of your pillow ,spiderstrewn
for *silence* drawing *silence* what abhors *ant* speech
,i speak *alone* to you who have forsaken breath
,my lov?e if love sur,vive s my ab,ject spee?ch my love
                        ;then i shall tell
                            what once occurred
            upon a certain day
                        too long too long ago.

                    know then, Constantine:
                                    whilst ocean-**S**evered

           you struggled in
           Armorica *ant*
           ,as i await
           ed ,all the burth
           en   of the Brythons'
           homeward fate
           upon me ,yearned
           alone but, strip
           ling *[Vortigern*
                freshbirthed
           and cradlebound
           nor knew you dead nor
           living we, ni
           ship and fraught
           there *came* to me
                on *ce*
       as I sur,rounded by
       my acolytes ,asleep: :my
       from *mirror, mirror* sheathed
       in dream in mist in thought
       in silver, runes enwreathed
       in rigor, moonlight caught
       as by a crafted sheen
       oft water *ant* caressed
       the moon a, mirror blessed
       a placid screen there wrought
   before me glitning or a subtle turn
   i gazed *ant*,   raptured, strove discerned
   ,inverted ,warped a, tangent face
   who stared nor un, fami liar ,one
   who watched *who,* slid *who,* stretched his hand
   through waterglass: a mirrorMan
   full straightly ,comely haunted
   youth ,did kiss me ,kiss him
   shard-eyed ,stunning , *void*, his trace
entrancing as the *void*, *void* mirrored there
and slicing glances flashing mirrorair

　　　　　(absolve me dear)
　　　　　　　　　his cold touch called forth flame—
and dreams ,and delicate desires:　came
in frisson nerving through my startled flesh
gnivol the, red shadowing in,cubus fresh
he reached *he* ,grasping through the runestrewn glass
caressed through, *me* the air *he*, slipped athwart *me*
from *me* mi,rr,ored ,ca *me* ,on jouâ *mes* ,clasped *we*
,arush my, blood with awe-borne lust and fear
and left me trembling ,joytossed.　　and the madness passed."

sad **C**onstantine
　　　　　was speechless; dim the drums above
thrummed, distant pulse of albion. thus sighed
　　　　grim Vivienne:
　　　　　　　　"(absolve me, dear)"
　　　　and then again:

　　　　　　　　　　　"my **L**ove,
the *void* is all-encompassing ,comme *love*
the mirror, depthless false ideal *lust* precise
like *love* ,the *void* the mirrorfolk *ant* vaast embrace
like *love* ,i feel the, still, the throbbing bliss the price
of living, *lust*, the *void* the ,felt it squirmed to *love* to life
i *love* the *void* the *void,* it came to me, its kiss of ice like lust
　　　(*absolve me dear*) in the shamanic night
　　　　　　　　—who issued from this fervour,
　　　　　　　　　　　　the secret:
　　　　　　　　　　　　the hyphen-
　　　　　　　　　　[coupled]
　　　　　　　　　　-ated one
　　　　　　　　　　　:the son
　　　　　　　　of Mirrors ,son
of albion through me *alone,* the son
(alas o Constantine, *not* sprung of thee)

                                    but
                        of one who cannot be:
            vanished descendent of an Absent one.
Ambrosius-Merlinus ,scion sworn to albion
's no son of yours, o corpse, though son to me.
            Ambrosius my seed my flesh:
    -*Merlinus* trace of disappearances:
                                    half menske
        l'androgyne of the spectral mesh
                                your loss,
            o C,nstantin,e. o Constan,tine
absolve ab,solve me wretched lov,e lo,ve Contant?ine
        solve solve, like glass in air o melt o
love o love or love."

            and **S**ilence draped oer Constantine
    ,and Vortigern as silent}.
                            silence s, trained
        like speech. and Vivienne knelt, deep aheed.

"so you **R**emain,"
            her voice was melted hush in her response; "you
                        sense ,cadaver
in your vert,igo the *void* you, lust ,ant mort
you slide you *love* you *void*ed Albion you *ants* you ,crushed
                    {*to a chillful joy}*
                    to the *lips* of
                            are not
                is not was not your *lust* the
                                        ver
            you know my *lust* my love in death
        you sway unmoved amidst the vaasting dark

                    encompassed wrapt in nothing
                invisible inspir ité
        voluptuous in *love* in *void* decay
                        kiss of the crouching earth
                            we find our ,ab
                                solution
                                ,mirror:death
            each differently apath, we cleave
together, aimant l'abyss, reflect or wormed
let us kiss the skin of absence like a flower
the blessreft interval
                            ,my l,ove my,
                lo,ve my,
        love."

and **V**ivienne fell silent as the dead the tomb.

            she laid
                    her teenful tears in a bed of earth
            and raised herselven ,soddenwise
            and breathed the debris of armies
            and braced against the cnillicht room
            and brushed *ant* loving cold *ant* wrist
            and shu dd, e   rr ,ed
and like an ancient bough bentnumbed by centuries she leaned
                and met his puckring stare his eyes
                    like sunken graves *ant* ,lids
                and blue, and whisp, she softly dre*ant*med
                    like a child that he breathed
            ant did not; *ant* she kissed *ant* love
                    like a brid*ant* kiss her*ant* love

        and she brushed them off , all of them ,crawling.

            and she was silent.
                she was silent
                he was silent
                she wassilent

LIX

                     s hewasilent
                      shewaslent
                       hewasent
                        hewaent
                        shewent
                         shwent
                          swent
                           sent
                Vortigern his, breathhooked]
                            at
         last sad Vivienne her, breath unhitched
                          turned
                                     away
her face a mirror of the death his face *ant* mirror ,d
blanched pale as the moon
                    she waned and wailed
                                         ,weeping

          ;and leaving left behind her like a **H**usk
             *her*love *her*hope *her*joy; and borne along
           she carried with *her*all *her*hatred keen
                against the bristled murders of the Real.
      and as she left she left behind *her*in *her*trust
                 unknown to *her, her*son—stunned Vortigern
        who shook and wondered at his mothers secret speech.
        a ghast a, swirling brynes he fled his mothers wrong
                       if wrong it was—at what
         he shrank from hearing like his fathers ,papery ,earen
                        :*his*brother *not*
                         *his*brother, *half*
                         a brother, *half*
                    a thing of light and thought
                           that cannot be
                            he shrank
      for love he loved his mother loved, his brother *(not*

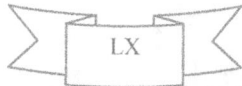

his brother)—yet to albion he pledged his love
and duty ,must remove this shard of absence
in the heart of albion, or must?—his broth
      er *(not his brother)*,dark ,inscrutible
      ,of sheer and parabolic thought—his
      brother *(not his brother)* who had taught
      him how to swallow light;—young Vortigern
stretched asunder, scraped twixt living love and duty to the dead
      ,and having weighed his futures in the dark
swore silence, loyal love, swore nothing should be said
of Vivienne's dread revel,ation naught be learned
of her sole shamesdeede, of Constantine's sole sorrow
nor of his brothers *(not his brothers)* tarnished name;
      he swore this to the darkness ,Vortigern
and to the silence of the barrow-bound. then turning round
          he gr,asped ,more firmly the gloaming rim
of *Wyrmwhit*, dented helm of albion assailed,
      and like a shadow slithered from the tomb
into the night of grim and flailing lamentations, loom
      of lamentations, albion's agony,
          and funereal deathclouds *lashed* with flame.

VI

~~~~~~

                "g,   'blinn shall I never
Ere my brain to-brist   or my breste other!
Was never sorrow so soft   that sank to my herte;
It is full sib to myself;   my sorr "

          -The Alliterative *Death of Arthur.*

~~~~~~

    The brythons gather and dance in a mad and frenzied ring around constantine's barrow, to the frantic noise of drums and flutes; on the crest of the barrow, his balefire blazes against the night sky. priests, singers and mourners from the four regions of Albion bring talismans of the elements to sacrifice to the flames, wailing ritual lamentations; they appeal to the deities to aid and usher constantine into his new place among the pantheon of Albion's emanations, where he will watch and bless his people silently, from a place of retirement, from within the Void between the words that speak what exists. at last each of his heirs leaves an offering of his own as a parting gift, followed by his consort vivienne, who offers a song of lamentation for constantine, and the fate of Albion.

Vivienne's Preludium to the Funereal Rites of Constantine

Henceforth you are blind, dear Constantine
    so i shall render to your withring eyes
you the roiling daunce
        the brythons have em,blazoned here
,where chaunts
          et weaving leaps and brands ablaze
            have wrought a temple ,sheer
    sans murs athwart the *vertices* of time
to render you into a deity ,*my dear.*

    my dear the stars flint punctures veer above
like drowning in the smokedrift ,warping air ,berweft
        above us ,*dear,* or crawling vault

        pleroma coiling *into into*
        all the archons fond aweep
        sky: vault of flame, flickerdancing
            with the torches shades
            bonfire lightbleeding

    ***F**or you, my farthing Constantine, my love*

    and walls of wailing ring the cloudsrwrirled sky
like babel raised ,vaast tangle in a single cry
for albion you were *dear* ,masonry of keening

    *for **Y**ou, my grotting Constantine, my love*

    and drumpound columns prop the dome aloft—
    the steadfast numbers shouldring tumult through
    —and boneshrill fluting chisels finials

    *for you, **M**y stielent Constantine, my love*

    while rushing round those plinths your people seethe
my dear, in anguish sea of, fleshflow ,monstrous wheel
        of torchlight fluid rush,ing
        relentless f,rothed in frenzy

    *for you, my **S**lournéd Constantine, my love*

    inside their circuit vaast expanse con ,tracts
of darkness shrinking or but onyx sea:
in its centre { ,*pupilwise,* } the tor
        glares at the gods
,*wound* in torchthrusts flaming , *bound*

in wovehair grief-shorn of the gathered thanes
and waiting your t,hree heirs (alas my, love)
        revolving round (

for you, my shuctain **C***onstantine, my love*

):the alter
        raised at the temp,les heart
        its heart twice-chambered, halved:
above :your balefire, lambent rose *abloom*
        atop your deathmound lain
        against the sky of bearhide
below :in earthen chamber bulging you, *my dear,*
        decay, metropolis of vermin
        ,love, and kiss
            not me
        but a vast abyss.

and spikepinned
    twin outcast
could you see ,*my dear,* here you would see
weary Vivienne , feral a, lone. she sings

for you, my slaispersed Constantine, my **L***ove, my love.*

The Mourning Dance of Constantine

~~~~~~~~~~~~~~~~~~~~~~~~~~~~~~~
" ere the first of all
whose whirling feet kept time
to the strict beat of the taut hide
and the squeal of the wailing flute.
Then fr "
-Euripides, *The Bacchae.*
~~~~~~~~~~~~~~~~~~~~~~~~~~~~~~~

the Mourning wheel ground the brythons in their dance awheel
in flame around the barrow ,nucleus of grislich keens of, chants
awaft with myrtlesmouken *bashed,* the dancers *pound* their, reel
snap twistarc sing whirl gnash awheel to the *drums* the *drumming*
clash and wailing ,spasmed in ,nor *drumming* ceaseless to the bloom
of death the, curled around the dead -king, *drummed* to dnuorg
bound up in ,fawnskin curling ,myrtle ,ivy-rapt in *pounding* ,hymn
four rings encircling *bashing* slapped the whirled, and feet kept time
the *drumming* spasmed neathe clouden, flames aspasméd in
drumming like, sparks reel snapgnash, twist whirl dancing wheel
the rasping wail of the shrill the, raving flute the *drums* the sparks flail
grasping gainst the dark atop the barrow bared, beneathe balefire
bleeding upward to the *drums* the *drumming* ,clouds astain
above the byrny torch-ring, *drum,* the barrow at its hub
an ant-mound bustling circlewise, aflame ,aroused
or mindless ,insectine stampede a flicker *drum* in circuit
slashing the grassy skin of albion draped in black in
nocturnal mourning the brythons shriek run spasmed whirl
they circle *drumbash* circling keening to the mite-crawled earen
of Constantine beloved, *drumming,* rushing circlewise they
nerve no thoughts to ,anguish *drumming* they, gallop frenetic, infernal
they fall, inrush they tangle fall, trample like ,corpses over corpses the
prayer of the limbs to the *drumming* to the, Aeons at play or ,at tentíve
above, aroused aflame at, rites, the sorrows of the earthen, people of dirt

who dance first in the dance the, *drumming* know no music, frantic flick
ring swarming feet of living, women men revealing mysteries
they, stung with frenzy hornet-like, the *drumming* drone
the *pounding*, thrashing, scintillant slow turning where the people
pounded, pul,ve, riséd in the grief of a,lbion, pressed to the *drums*
the *drum* the, funeral of Constantine: *drumming drumming*
sacred wheel en feu, en flamme, *pound* whirled grinding *drumming*
pound into meal the thanes of albion , *drumming drumming drumming*

like **S**cattring chaff:

        and **C**onstantine was silent.

Vivienne's Dirge and Prayer of the Brythons for Constantine

1

From the foliage-rustled wealds
consume,d with zeal
brand'shing oak flam,beaux we kneel
o *Constantine* o
{beaconspak of Brythons   ,fumant-seal}
and weep.

2

from the tirip-sucking fens
we bear thew, illow hence
with water sooth,e freshet cleanse
o *Constantine* o
{balm of Brythons solvent   ,mend}
and weep.

3

from the skin-thrashredding moors
we rush wit,h what is yours
wind whisp, ring fate or roar
o *Constantine* o
{word of Brythons   ,brise breath-soare}
and weep.

4

from the tooth-cracked crags et tors
we bear an,d dirt endure
beneath eht ear,then mantle worn
o *Constantine* o
{corps des Brythons   ,gendered forth}
and weep.

Chorus:

on the verd,ant swell the plain
alembi,c all contain
solvio all in ele,mental rain
o *Constantine* o
{sembled Brythain sol ,mourns wane}
and weep ,and ash and rend our hair

1

o weep, weep, for Constantine :birth-bound S,ire of Brythons
for he weeps alone.
o *weep*, weep, for Constantine :Sin,ging Glut-Blade
for he weeps alon.e
o weep, *weep*, for Constantine :Ward of Un,begettings
for he weeps alo.ne
o weep, weep, *for* Constantine :of the sundim t,ower
for he weeps al.one
in Avalon

2

o weep, weep, for *Constantine* :Piger,adamic Mould
for he weeps a.lone
o weep, weep, *for* Constantine :Thyrsic Spear of Gene,ration
for he weeps .alone
o weep, *weep*, for Constantine :Initial of the Sign,ified Seed
for he weeps. alone
o *weep*, weep, for Constantine :Desp,oiler of Archonic Edens
for he weep.s alone
in Avalon

3

o weep, weep, for Constantine :M,ask of the Pale Monad
for he wee.ps alone
o *weep*, weep, for Constantine :glowrin,g Sol-Helm

                    for he we.eps alone
o weep, *weep*, for Constantine :Emblazoned with Just,ice
                    for he w.eeps alone
o weep, weep, *for* Constantine :of the Cliff-Hung Cour,t
                    for he .weeps alone
                        in Avalon

4

o weep, weep, for *Constantine* :garnished with p,ungent laurels
                    for he. weeps alone
o weep, weep, *for* Constantine :Bristling Ox of the ,,,Shield-Wall
                    for h.e weeps alone
o weep, *weep*, for Constantine :Stoi,c Scribe of eht Ages
                    for .he weeps alone
o *weep*, weep, for Constantine :Slake,r of the Blood of Rome
                    for. he weeps alone
                      in Avalon

Chorus:

o weep, weep, for Constantine :Para,gon of Frekest Thanes
                    fo.r he weeps alone
o *weep*, weep, for Constantine :Vessel of Calliop,e
                    f.or he weeps alone
o weep, *weep*, for Constantine :Her,oic Voice of Peoples
                    .for he weeps alone
o weep, weep, *for* Constantine :Out,cast Parnassian
                    for he weeps alone.
                      in Avalon
                       ,*dead.*

    weeping we implore, o deities
                    { o *dead*}

you Bless grim Constantine ,we:
implore strict urizen, great los
,samael ap yaldabaoth
spark-aborted, known
as sakla also; sol
ablaze, and lambent luna
—elsewise artemis
and helios, or paired
apollo and diana!
,o beulah, brân, o galatea,
twice-named ,in stream and marble
,and blodeuwedd, lillyskinned
,crypted hastur, belenus,
bacchus, lugh, medea,
leutha ,lovely isis
, llud the son of beli
mawr ,of mickle spawn
(who llyr and dôn begat)
;to vala too, and taliesin
,and enitharmon ,grinning
nayarlathotep ,branwen
the fair, pygmalion,
glewlwydd the grasper
and dagon ,fishbred! to
the leper king in bells
and lucifer, to luvah, orc
,wise seth ,and scorched
prometheus ,athoth
,grainhaired amæthon
,culhwch ,astaphaios
,all the archons, pitched
with anger, homunculi,
manawythan, and molech
and mathônwy of the waves,
the shoggoths leering dim
,to eleleth ,cthulu ,thel

,hermes triple-gendered,
and abel ,harmas of
the jealous eyen, ulro,
eurydice and enion
,nebro ,shub niggurath,
goat of the thousand young,
with gracklefaffin snapping
and gwyn-ap-nudd, abron
and tharmas, gwydion
,englaimed demigorgon
,govannan iron-armed
,boudica, narcissus
,and cain! o -king in yellow,
sabaoth, and orpheus
of the lyre, oothoon
and to the streaming naiads
and dryades swaying, cold
cassilda ,onorthochras
icarus ,yog sothoth,
ysbaddaden savage,
lonely alastor ,and
ashtoroth ,and mournful
slight ahania, and to
annwn grim gatewarder,
gwyrthur son of the scorch

,and you
    who wear the pallid mask, enigma, we implore:

welcome Constantine into the *realm* of **D**eath
    among the sun,dered pantheon
his name parchment-scraped, palimpsest for albion
    's future script, to bless it
    from the place where he has
        { *not* } wit,hdrawn
    ,in Avalon!

tamp down Constantine into the wormfed loam
           far from the sund,ered pantheon
his carnal selven, corpse to compost fed for albion
               's nourishment, to bless
               us with the body *bb*wn
                   in his decay
                   ,in Avalon!

conduct great Constantine into the blaze of day
               among the sunde,red pantheon
his dreaming cloudwise to the tome of albion
               's epic sky-leaf writ, to bless
               its dissipation, drift
                   in sol,vent light
                   ,in Avalon!

erase from Constantine the man who ,ruled
               among the s,undered pantheon
for,ego his life ,that was ;what was not gr,*ant* to albion
               's hope, from death to bless
               un,born *un*,sought joys
                   absent *in* joined
                   ,*in* Avalon!

embroider Constantine into the womb of words
               among the sunder,ed pantheon
a deity of, shifting , passed to poemythic albion
               's chorus, voiceless bless
               -ing, chariot of ventures
                   sooth e in prophesy
                   ,ensconced in Avalon!

Uther:

my **F**ather

    i carry cains of *wheat* from seed sweat-won
        from the soil ,tithe to *Tharmas*
    and with it all repose i render you
        in death ,who rested never
    nor shall i rest ere death; through toil grew
        *your*reign, in work *your*fruit *your*son
        :burn, grain-cackling!
        for Constantine is dead

Vortigern:

my **F**ather,

    i bear fresh *flesh*-fat, amen abel fare
        to purchase prayers for *Urizen*,
    the pity plucked from ,me i, pass to you
        ,in death, who wept never
    oer needful pains; the stare all treachors rue
        i'll share goresmeared, aglare
        :burn, ice-searing!
        for Contantine is dead

Ambrosius-Merlinus:

my **M**aster

    i seth ere before you but a whisp ered word
        :my secret *name*, oblation to *Los*: i
    renounce it ,never spoken, for i leave to you
        in death ,who lived never
    but cleftwise centreless ,whom none but knew
        stray facets: *Self*—my own, interred

:burn, thought-blazing!
the Pen-Dragon is dead

Vivienne:

my Love,

our nuptial *torque* this eve n,ing i bring
for *Luvahs* final litanies;
serpent-twinned ,my love i leave to you
in death, who scorned it n,ever
:my joy, enringed here y,ours though wrought for two
for naught remains but blades and kings
:burn, past-ashing!
for Constantine my love is dead

Chorus:

Our pen-dragon,

bound in samite
swithe sagging into soil
pendragon ,dead
corrupted in the Real
spiral, and spark:
we commit you to the void
we commit you to the void
we commit you to the void
we thrust the spear of albion ,*Rhongomyniad*
into *Urthona's* ravening flame
your carcasse en fumée to, char withern you
and we commit you to the void
we commit you to the void
we commit you to the void
dead Constantine
til *Rhongomyniad* thrusts grellid forth anew

     privé til germination ,
       ça ressed by rain
       enrayed in season
   of death, who dropped it never
until your graveworms sculpt a shoot
       (dead Constantine)
      of wood and sap
       { slim thyrsus }
      stripling spear
you wielded in advance we, yield
      :burn, shaft spark-winging!
    for Constantine is dead
and we commit him to the void
   Constantine is dead
and we commit him to the void
 we commit him to the void
   Constantine is dead
and we commit him to the void
we commit him to the void
we commit him to the void
   Constantine is dead
and we commit him to the void
we commit him to the void
we commit him to the void
we commit him to the void
   Constantine is dead
and we commit him to the void
we commit him to the void
we commit him to the void
we commit him to the void
we commit him to the void
   Constantine is dead

woe, woe to albion
     :the wind is bleeding.

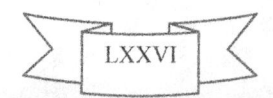

The Lament of Vivienne for Her Love

~~~~~~~~~~~~~~~~~~~~~~~
" n my bed at night
I sought him who my soul loves.
I sought him, but found him not;
I called him, but he gave no answer.
I will rise now and go a "
  -*Song of Solomon*
~~~~~~~~~~~~~~~~~~~~~~~

alas I seek my love in the stud ded fields

       yet he vanishes at my fingerbrus,h
 i seek my love in the looming deep
       yet he sssinks from my pitching prow
 i seek my love on the tust led tors
       yet he w,hisks into the gnashing wind
alas i seek, to lose my love
       slain by what Exists

alas I seek my love in beetling, shadows

       yet he slides from t,he shades
 i seek my love in echoes thhrumminng
       yet he hides in silences
 i seek my love in lingered fragrances
       yet he mingles with the dust
alas i seek to lose, my love
       slain by what Exists

alas I seek my love in the fringes of ,my eyen

       yet he fl,ashes from view
 i seek my love in a w aking sweat
       yet he flees my palpitating lids
 i seek my love in twixt the ink and p,age

                yet he dries and ,yellow fades
alas i seek to lose my love,
          slain by what Exists

alas **I** seek my love in fit,ful memory
            yet he shrivels s,toneward
   i seek my love in his crypt below
          yet he *rus*∆es to live
   i seek my love within my very love
          yet embrace an abyss
alas, i seek to lose my love
    i seek to lose my love

{alas i sought i seek my love in, runetched glass
     my love i lost me , thus in mirror
flected into love i cannot ,lie
     with me i find my love in glass}

     my love you l   eave me sliced
       and heved   ed in hie
         you dy   ad i
                   al
                   one
   and where
    you were
    the world
  *en*croach es

     born *into* what, is
     where,*in* is death
            my dear

        i am gutted of tears
     if i weep i shall weep dust
no more my love must i nor weep for you
     ,slain by what Exists

:a clutch-of **D**ooms for every heir of albion:

and so my, love as love, i lock with you below
$\qquad\qquad\qquad$ soil to flesh
and so my, love as rage, burns into from y our kindled
$\qquad\qquad\qquad$ in *your*
$\qquad\qquad\qquad$ in fern o
$\qquad\qquad$ blazoned forth
$\qquad$:slain by what Exists

behold my love my locks of raveng ,flame
behold my love my fury-furr,owed brow
behold my love my poison-bladed ,eyes
behold my love my cheeks cast fa *mine*-shadows
behold my love my nostrils flame-fla,red
behold my love the razorbridge that par,ts them
behold my love my ears that ,cradle in their curls a storm
behold my love my lips like blood
$\qquad$ for my love is dead, in avalon

behold my love my neck a, sturdy to,wer
behold my love my bat tered shoulder-cliffs
behold my love my spine that b ristles to the breezeblast
behold my love my ribs vice-grasping all my heavemoansobs
behold my love my breasts like shields braced
behold my love my nipples ,spikes at the real's vein
behold my love my waist ten,der as a snails throat
behold my love my hips ,brittle ships sun-b leached
$\qquad$ for my love is dead, in avalon

behold my love my thighs like mantis limbs
behold my love my knees like sup,pliant barna clés
behold my love my calves like drown,ed swans
behold my love my sh,ins like crumbleledges
behold my love my ankles ,dolor-wrench ed
behold my love my feet like salmon flattttened

behold my love my toes like tu mors
    for my love is dead, in avalon

behold my love my ar,ms like statues arms that c,r,ack
behold my love my el,bows skin-worn thru
behold my love the vein th,at sings so aeerily
behold my love my wrists that wri,the loss
behold my love my ,hands wormbitten books
behold my love my fingers twi sting like medusa's scalp
behold my love my nails like tombstones of pearl
    for my love is dead, in avalon

behold my love my womb con,vulses your deathrattles
behold my love my arteries ,scald and lavascorched
behold my love my nerves pluck glas,s
behold my love my mind its, miasmatic phlegm
behold my love my brea,th rent a;nguish-hooked
behold my love my voice that rasp-whips sand
behold my love my tongue-kracken ,stranded tooth-torn ,beached
    for my love is dead, in avalon
        slain by what Exists

    o Constantine **O** Constantine
        i come to seize my ,leave:

    aaa*aaa*aaaa*a*aaaa*aaa*aaaaaa

      a*aaa*a*aaa*aaaa*aaa*aaa*aaaa*aa*aa*aaa*a

chance-**S**las*h*ed and rag*g*ed with dishevel *i* approach
,my love
sho*rn* like ashes *wretch*ed writhing greyblade windswept like
,my love
my mind a moor parchedwept athirst i *tri*ckle tears at *t*ongue
,my love

words words unheard in Avalon

eeeeeeeeeeeeeeeeeeeeeeeeeeeeeeeeee

eeeeeeeeeeeeeeeeeeee

and **W**herefore lash my nerv and-moorings snapping froughtful sobs
,my love
your lip hand kiss chest hip your hair em*brace* rib ardour arm throat throb
,my love
your bellowvoicing ,whispered ,satin sigh my madness speaks like you
,my love

words words unheard in Avalon

iiiiiiiiiiiiiiiiiiiiiiiiiiiiiiiiiiiiiiiiiiiiiiii

iiiiiiiiiiiiiiiiiiiiiiiiiiiiiiiiiiiiiiiiiii

what crud ataf **S**napped saw-slaked at unsæn where now i watch
,my love
i watch three our assassination sons and twoo yet *still* he loves nor yet the edge
,my love
a bone fray *thr*eading albion your touch you *smiled* guard to grow to kill
,my love

words words unheard in Avalon

oooooooOOOOOOOOOOOOOOoooo

oooOOOOooooooOOOOOoooooooo

no **M**ore to slip your waken honeyed syntax tongue to press nor speak
,my love
ne venture teach them *soft* ne bounding poetry of greeting nor to ask

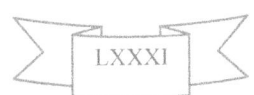

,my love
nor feel you thinking on the skin to *strength* discerning stroke or sing
,my love

       word*s* *w*ords unheard in Avalon

       uu*uuuUUUuuuuuu*

       uuu*uUUuuuuuuuUUuUUU*uu*uuUuuuu*

henceforth you are a **V**oid to *sw*allow *all* of *us* you love we lose

,my love

henceforth a shadow *drap*ing stri*v*e star drawing *g*uard thought vortex go

,my love

pen-dragon s*t*riding kindly furl the cliff wrath branches gone but *fruit*

,my love

and ter*r*ors striven str*ew*n the stars i *see* as vales carrion gagged fleece

,my love

and yea*r*s per smo*t*ken *plague* i fear i watc*h* across nor sh*ie*ld-wall

,my love

but albion shall flail froth cor*rupt* aga*i*nst itselvensplit reft wretch

,my love

henceforth you *a*re our future *g*aped ghost-*breathed* our blindness s*w*ord

,my love

hence*f*orth are nothing you but *a*lbion its unguessed course its *f*ear must be

,my love

no sha*d*ow breath but albion you *stalk* as albion emb*r*ace not but as albion

,my love

erased in *terr*ed your laugh your pause glance al*l* but s*t*rength in albion alone

,my love

so safeguard albion or stri*k*e for albion my *batt*elove alone is left of love for you

,my love

for all of yo*u* is dead lest albion prey to the Real *fall* thus love kills *l*ove to live

,my love

of albion the daemon you of albion the *sign* and m*us*e of albion of albion of all

,my love

you are to all to albion the a*b*sent patron al*b*ion to all to me alone to me alone to me alone

,my love

i **C**ommit you to the void

i commit you to the void

      skincracked cadaver

      you are it is a

      seed a *seed* ,my love and

i commit it to the void

i commit you to the void

      the void *my* love *is*

      seething soil ,womb

        of futures and

i commit you to the void

i commit you to the void

      i plant you ,love,

      in awe ,ful loam

      in no thing in

      silent albion

      { *nutrient abyss* }

to fallow there a gene

      ration ,curled away

from the wrack of torment albion

      to slice when the sun reflames

      through the Reals skin

aaaeuaaiiaauaeeeiieoeeieeeoeeeuei

iiüiiiiiiaiiiioieiiooOaoouoouuuauiuuu

fare **W**ell *my*, Constan,tine , *my* love *my* love

      slain by what Exists

i commit you to the void

o *myrtlesmoken ,bathed in ash* o

i commit you to the void

Constantine *my* si,lent love

set jewel-like midst, the sundered pantheon
henceforth you weep alone in avalon
        you who wept, never

        for **Y**ou are dead
    slain by what Exists
and i commit you to the void
i commit you to the void
i see,k you love and you are dead
so i commit you to the void
i commit you to the void
i seek to lose my love, my love
so i commit you to the void
i commit you to the void
i commit you to the void
    slain by what Exists:
behold my voice-clenched word ,love
    behold our heirs my ,love
      pen-dragons fierce in ,love
be,hold our bitter purpose ,love:

we
    pen-dragons:

uther vortigern ambrosius-merlinus , **L**ove

and i my love and your dead seed we plant tonight here from our love
whom i shall consecrate and husband though i die to see him born
,my love
whom seed passed through your seed must be conceived to grasp your dream
,my love
thrice three years hence to wreak our vengeance gainst the world that Is
,my love
whom i shall name tonight to haunt unborne the flesh of what Exists
,my love

: **A**rthur :

fut*ur*e thane of **A**lbion

in de*a*th we drea*m* of you to ,night

sle*e*p ,you who sha*l*l be

when a*l*l of us

Pen-d*ragons*

shall rot *by* the side of star-mo*urn*ed Constantin*e*

{*o* Constantine my, lo*ve* my love}

Arthur :

yo*u* the

yet un*b*orn—you

shall make the Real ,bleed.

www.ingramcontent.com/pod-product-compliance
Lightning Source LLC
Chambersburg PA
CBHW080601090426
42735CB00016B/3305